STORIES OF KRISHNA

A PROJECT OF THE DHARAM HINDUJA INSTITUTE OF INDIC RESEARCH FACULTY OF DIVINITY, UNIVERSITY OF CAMBRIDGE

3

I N D I C
V A L U E S
S E R I E S

VIVIENNE
BAUMFIELD

Bayeux Arts

SERIES EDITOR:
JULIUS LIPNER

Stories of Krishna
Vivienne Baumfield
© Copyright 2000, Bayeux Arts, Inc.

Published by

Bayeux Arts Inc.

119 Stratton Crescent S.W.
Calgary, Alberta, Canada T3H 1T7

Design: Brian Dyson, Syntax Media Services

Canadian Cataloguing in Publication Data

Baumfield, Vivienne
Stories of Krishna

(Indic Values Series; 3)
ISBN 1 896209-37-8

1. Krishna (Hindu Deity) I. Title II. Series
BL1220.B38 2000   294.5'2113   C00-910214-0

The publisher gratefully acknowledges the generous support of The Alberta Foundation for the Arts, The Canada Council for the Arts, and the Government of Canada through the Book Publishing Industry Development Program.

Printed in Hong Kong by King's Times Printing

To Dermot Killingley,
who first inspired my interest
in the Indian Tradition — VB

Contents

Editor's Preface

The first volume of this *Series* (now renamed the *Indic Values Series*) appeared in July 1997. It was called *Sita's Story* and was published to wide acclaim. The second volume, entitled *Guru Nanak*, has recently been published. This, the third volume, maintains the high standards of its predecessors. Krishna is a central figure of divinity in the Hindu tradition. Portrayed in a variety of ways - as a majestic teacher, an ardent lover, an endearing child, a consuming God - it is instructive to inquire into what the traditions are saying about him, and into the different ways his devotees approach him. This will give us a glimpse not only into the complexity of Hinduism but also into the richness and variety of human ways of self-understanding and self-transcendence. This book initiates us into a consideration of these various topics.

The aim of this *Series* is to explore and inform about its various subjects in a way that is accessible to a wide public, from teenagers to adults of all communities, South Asian as well as other. The authors are all experts in their fields, and are experienced in explaining sometimes difficult material in a fair-minded, objective but insightful manner. Thus it is also hoped that teachers of Religious Education and Religious Studies will find this *Series* helpful.

Dr Vivienne Baumfield is well-qualified to write this book. She took her PhD in Indian studies at the University of Newcastle upon Tyne, where she lectures in the Department of Education. She is responsible for training Primary and Secondary students to teach Religious Education, and has taught Religious Education in state secondary schools for 13 years. Dr Baumfield is Vice Chair of the Religious Education Council for England and Wales, and Associate Editor of the *British Journal of Religious Education*.

Further volumes in this *Series* are now in preparation, and some forthcoming titles are given on the back cover of this book.

Dr Julius Lipner, Director,
Dharam Hinduja Institute of Indic Research,
Faculty of Divinity, University of Cambridge,
September, 1999

Author's Preface

This book invites you to reflect upon the questions the stories of Krishna raise, and to consider their relevance for us today. The book is organised around two central and devotional texts, the *Bhagavad Gita* and the *Bhagavata Purana*, and the contributions of some Hindus in Newcastle upon Tyne, England, who are devotees of Krishna. It is called *Stories of Krishna* because any attempt to present one "essential" story of Krishna would be misguided as it is through exploring the diversity of Krishna-stories and their apparent contradiction that understanding of the significance of Krishna grows. It is by the re-telling and re-interpretation of the stories in different contexts and in different generations that they become meaningful. I hope that you will formulate what Krishna means for you as you read this book and consider the questions it raises for you.

I would like to thank the people who gave so generously of their time and were prepared to share their understanding of Krishna. What they told me is recorded in their own words in the first chapter, and, as you will see, influences the train of thought in the rest of the book.

Note for Teachers: The various Questions for reflection and discussion raised in the course of the text are some of those that came to mind after working on this book, and are intended to act as a guide for teachers and to stimulate further thought and discussion in the classroom, for Hindus and non-Hindus alike. At the end of the book teachers will find further suggestions for guidance towards a deeper grasp of the material discussed.

Note on Names and Terms: Names and terms which appear in **bold** type are explained in the **Glossary** at the end of the book. Sanskrit or other non-English terms (including names of texts) are given in *italics*. Those words that are listed in the Glossary occur in bold type only on their first occurrence.

Dr Vivienne Baumfield,
Department of Education,
University of Newcastle upon Tyne,
August, 1999

Introduction

The stories discussed in this book are mainly from two key texts, the *Bhagavad Gita* and the *Bhagavata Purana*, and from interviews with members of the local Hindu community in Newcastle upon Tyne, UK, for whom Krishna is an important figure. It would be impossible to do justice to the rich heritage of stories in a short book, and to reduce the variety to one "essential" or "basic" story would be misguided as one thing we learn from Krishna is to value diversity. So what you will find is an exploration of the themes arising from the personal insights and experiences of people who would describe themselves as followers of Krishna in our contemporary world. It is the intention of this book to stimulate an interest which will lead you to explore the rich cultural heritage of Krishna for yourself. Hopefully, the exploration will be guided by a willingness to engage with the stories and to ask the question: *What does Krishna mean today?* In the course of this book I have raised a number of more specific questions based on my understanding of the stories of Krishna. I will have succeeded in my task if you can contribute many more.

Chapter 1
Stories of Krishna: a Conversation between generations

What is your image of Krishna? Is it the richly dressed young man playing his flute in the forests around Vrindaban in northern India or by the banks of the sacred river Yamuna (also written Jumna)? Paintings, poetry, dance and music tell the story of this playful figure charming his followers. *But is there one story or are there many stories?*

We can find stories of Krishna as a child, as a cowherd, as a prince in a palace or a charioteer on the battlefield. The stories of Krishna have been handed on to us across the centuries and each time we hear them, we are invited to respond and try to understand what the message is for us. It is a conversation between the generations as parents pass on the stories to their children so that they can enjoy them and learn, and then pass them on in turn. The world would be a chaotic and dangerous place if we were left to rediscover everything for ourselves, and yet each one of us brings something new as we listen to the stories.

The people who have contributed their stories of Krishna to this book want to play their part in the conversation. For them, the stories of Krishna are a precious gift. They hope that what they have to say will encourage you to find out more about Krishna and think about what he might have to say to you and your generation. That is why we begin this book by listening to devotees of Krishna. It will give us an idea of the different ways Krishna can influence his followers' lives.

Dr Nath

> Dr Nath was born in Hospet, Karnataka State in southern India, and has lived in the UK since 1969. He is a GP in Stanley, a small town in County Durham, where he lives with his wife and two daughters. Dr Nath has a special interest in trying to understand the **Gita** and the **Upanishads** and explaining their meaning to others. He gives weekly lectures on the *Gita* at the **mandir** (temple) and frequently holds discussion groups.

Dr Nath says: "In Hinduism, religious ideas are brought out into the minds of children

Krishna playing the flute.

from their early days. This is done through stories from the **Puranas** and the great epics, the *Ramayana* and *Mahabharata*. Some of these stories become deeply embedded in the minds of children and they continue to think about them as they get older. Pictures are also associated with many of the stories and through their symbolism many abstract ideas can be explored. I want to concentrate on three pictures which illustrate stories showing important aspects of Krishna: as a child, Bala Krishna; as a cowherd, Gopala Krishna; and as the teacher in the *Gita*, Jagad-Guru Krishna.

Bala Krishna steals the butter

This is one of Krishna's childhood pranks when because of his love of butter, he attempts to steal some from the householders of Gokula, where he grew up. When children hear the story from the *Bhagavata Purana* they are drawn to Krishna because of the humour and naughtiness but the story also has a deeper meaning that we can come to understand as we grow older.

Butter is made from the milk produced by cows. It is not visible, although present in the milk, until it has been churned. Cows are regarded as sacred in Hinduism because they represent the scriptures, called **Vedas***;* so the milk is the *Vedas*. The churning represents the refinement of the *Vedas* in the *Upanishads* and the butter is the truth, the essential understanding of creation-existence-destruction. Butter is tasty and we all enjoy it just as the truth is beautiful and something we all seek. Bala Krishna's love of butter signifies his love for *sat-chid-ananda*, that is, truth-knowledge-bliss.

Gopala Krishna and the *gopis*

Another prank of Krishna as a young man is when he comes across some **gopis** (milkmaids) bathing in a pool. He sneaks up, takes their sarees and climbs up a nearby tree to wait for them to finish bathing. In this story, also from the same Purana, the *gopis* represent desire and show that all desires must lead us towards the feet of the Lord. Desire must drop its covering (the *gopis'* sarees) which is the ego and move towards the truth. We must approach the Lord stripped of our ego, naked, and turn our desire towards attaining **moksha** or liberation from worldliness if we are to reach the feet of our Lord.

Krishna in the tree, receiving the *gopis'* homage.

Jagad Guru Krishna: *Gitopadesha* **(The Teaching of the** *Gita***)**

Krishna, as his disciple Arjuna's charioteer, represents the journey of life as a chariot ride. Our only constant companion is the charioteer as everything else - family and friends - falls away at different stages on the journey. The horses are like our desires which pull us along but they need a firm steer if they are to take us in the right direction. The reins are our mind and all will be secure if our minds are on Krishna just as the reins are in his hands as the charioteer. If we trust in Krishna, he will lead us and teach us so that we choose the right course of action. Arjuna is very confused and depressed at the beginning of the *Gita* and throws down his bow but when he has accepted the advice of his charioteer, the teachings of Krishna, he is able to take up his duties. The story teaches us that those who surrender their mind to Krishna overcome mental weakness and despair and are able to fulfill their duty".

Veena Soni

Veena Soni is a primary school teacher in Newcastle. She co-ordinates Religious Education in her school and also works with the bilingual pupils. Veena represents the local Hindu community on the group responsible for monitoring Religious Education in the city and often visits schools to talk to teachers about the Hindu tradition. She has been involved in trying to set up classes for Hindu children so that they can learn more about their tradition. Her father was one of the founding members of the *mandir* which began life in the front room of a terraced house.

Veena Soni says: "Stories of Krishna as a child are very human and show him doing all the kinds of things any real, normal child would do and yet at the same time they contain important teachings. I use stories of Krishna with my own children to teach them about **dharma** or right conduct. It is possible to select stories according to the age of the child. Krishna as a baby suits young children and as they grow they can relate to teachings about friendship or family relationships through stories of Krishna, his brother Balarama and their friends. The stories are helpful in showing what our duties are in different situations; for example, his relationship with his real mother and his adopted mother can be a very important lesson for children. By the time a child is 17 or 18 years old they are ready to study the *Bhagavad Gita*.

Krishna in the war-chariot with Arjuna.

Many of our festivals are associated with Krishna and often involve acting out aspects of the stories. Through the celebrations the warmth, energy and colourful nature of Krishna is demonstrated in a way that is enjoyable to children and the whole family. As well as the festivals, we find the TV serials and videos of the *Mahabharata* have helped to convey the stories of Krishna to our children. We can sit down as a family and enjoy the stories and children can identify with Krishna because he is such an attractive figure. I find that children are able to compare themselves with incidents in Krishna's life so that their understanding of *dharma* grows; they can make the link themselves. I feel it is important for the next generation that we find a way of passing on the stories so that they continue to see that they have an importance and relevance in their lives.

Women I find have an affection for Krishna who plays an important part in their family life, particularly in the teaching of their children and the celebration of festivals. There is not the same intensity in their feelings towards **Shiva** who is more awe-inspiring as the protector of family life. Krishna is a friend and a guide. He is friendly and accessible even though one big difference between Krishna and the previous incarnation as **Ram** is that he always knew that he was God whilst Ram did not realise this until he slew the demon **Ravan**.

I would say that for 90% of Hindus Krishna is the *Bhagavad Gita*. It is the most important thing about Krishna because it rescues people and lays down the principles of Hinduism. We have many prayers and celebrations to mark this great gift from Krishna whom we respect as the supreme teacher and who, through the *Gita*, sets us an example of how to live and relate to other people. Krishna is the last of the great incarnations of God and he came to pass on the teachings which should guide our lives.

As I have grown up I have changed in my view of God so that I now think more in terms of an energy or power which takes the form of each incarnation as a deity. I find it difficult to say that I prefer this one or that one. Unlike some people who link with one form of God, I draw values from each incarnation because I see God as the energy taking different forms. People choose their own image of God according to their particular needs and personality but in the end they all have the same source".

Hari Shukla

Hari Shukla was born in Kampala, Uganda. He taught in primary schools in Uganda and Nairobi, Kenya, before moving to Britain in 1973. The following year he was offered the post of Director of Tyne and Wear Racial Equality

Characters from the TV version of the *Mahabharata*.

Krishna and Arjuna: a scene from the *Bhagavad Gita*.

Council based in Newcastle, and settled there with his family. Hari has devoted his life to the promotion of partnership between ethnic minority communities and the creation of a multi-cultural society in which every individual's contribution is valued. He chairs many local organisations concerned with inter-faith relationships, education and other concerns.

Hari Shukla says: "I think of Krishna as an incarnation of God, following on from the previous incarnations of **Vishnu**, which include Lord Rama: God who has three functions as the creator, sustainer and destroyer. Krishna is very important to me because of the precious gift he brought - the *Bhagavad Gita*. The message of the *Gita*, Krishna's teaching to Arjuna, is very relevant today as attachment to material things and confusion about the right way to act are big problems in our society. Through the *Gita*, Krishna gives a framework for us to live a purposeful and fulfilling life and he does it in a way that leaves us free to decide for ourselves. There is no force, simply an example of how it could be. Krishna helps us to understand by explaining every aspect of life carefully. In the *Gita* we learn about the law of **karma** and the necessity of controlling the *gunas* or basic constituents of material and mental life so that we can allow our best qualities to lead us. The importance of trust as the key factor in all human relationships is the lesson to be learned from the relationship between Arjuna and Lord Krishna. You do your best and Krishna sorts out the rest. Your best is based on faith, which is essentially obedience, and the right intention from the heart. If you will put your trust in Krishna, then he will look after you and give you the wisdom you need. The Gita shows how the ego is a barrier to success because it destroys trust. The lesson Arjuna has to learn as he struggles to understand his duty is the essential truth that we all must come to understand: whatever I am is not because of me but because of Him.

Krishna teaches a very practical religion, a way of life, and young people first come to understand his teachings through family relationships which should model and "live" the *Gita*. The concept of service is very important in the *Gita* and we should see whatever we have as a gift from Krishna and exercise **prashad** by sharing with others. The community is very important for Hindus because it is through living for others that we become our true selves. Helping other people is a privilege and whenever an opportunity to be kind presents itself, we should say, "Thank you God for including me".

Krishna is a living God and we can talk to him. He is approachable and there are

Devotees of Krishna.

many ways of encountering Krishna; as he teaches in the *Gita*, "It doesn't matter what name you call me". This flexibility appeals to young people because it doesn't set up divisions but encourages acceptance of different points of view, different faiths. Krishna outlines three ways of attaining *moksha* and any one of them will get you there. People who follow the teachings of the *Gita* are good citizens and can easily find a place in the wider community".

Dr Anand

Dr Anand has a medical practice in a suburb of Newcastle. He was born in Bihar State in India where he attended a Catholic Secondary school. Whilst he was still in India, he studied with a guru and came to a deeper understanding of the Hindu tradition and the person of Krishna. He is a talented musician, a flautist, and plays both Western and Indian classical music.

Dr Anand says: "My first thoughts of Krishna come through a reaction to the stern character of Rama. With Rama the emphasis on right and wrong leads to a pre-occupation with punishment which, I feel, is unduly harsh. Krishna is quite the opposite and teaches love, acceptance, tolerance. He is soft and compassionate, very feminine as opposed to Rama as masculine. When we think of Krishna we are charmed by his wealth and beauty; he is associated with music and carries a flute as opposed to Rama's bow. As a musician, I can identify with Krishna as an artist who uses beauty, music and poetry to communicate with us. He is democratic and not concerned with hierarchies; Rama had Hanuman, the monkey devotee, as a servant but Krishna has no servants. Krishna is the nicer side of us, the side that brings happiness and a sense of fun so that life is not seen as a chore but something to enjoy.

The model of family life presented by Krishna and **Radha** is less stereotypical than that of Rama and **Sita**; it is more open and we get a sense that he valued the company of his wife who was also his friend. In fact, the family relationships are closer to ordinary life because they are more human. Stories of Krishna span from his childhood through to adulthood showing different aspects of his complex personality so that he can be a role model for what I want to be, for what is appropriate for me at a particular time in my life. Krishna appeals to us in different contexts. I think that our understanding of God evolves, changes as we change, so that, in a way, we create God.

One incident in Krishna's life I often think about is the battle scene at the beginning of the *Bhagavad Gita* where Arjuna throws down his bow. Arjuna can be any one of us when we stand at a cross-roads in our life with the powers of good and evil balanced and a difficult choice to make. Krishna is important to us when we face real dilemmas, situations which may require us to "kill our gurus" so that we can move on to a new level of understanding, assume new responsibilities. When it is necessary Krishna will teach and lead. In the *Gita* he talks straight but without heaviness or anger and shows us that it is possible to be honest, even say harsh things, without hurt but with sweetness. It is through his compassion that Krishna enables us to take on our responsibilities.

The story of the two trees and the friend who eats the fruit teaches us that guilt is not important. In the story, Krishna's friend is unable to stop himself from eating the fruit from the best of the two trees and afterwards is ashamed of what he has done but

Krishna and Radha in Vrindavan

Krishna is not annoyed with him. Just as the boy Krishna does not blame his friend for taking the fruit, so we need not feel blamed or guilty when we make a wrong choice in our lives. Krishna's spirituality is not heavy or unduly serious; we have duties and responsibilities which we should fulfill but we need not take ourselves too seriously. Krishna is playful but testing".

Dhananjai

Dhananjai is a Western convert to Hinduism and a member of ISKCON (the International Society for Krishna Consciousness), more popularly known as the "Hare Krishnas". He is based at the centre in Newcastle which has a small group of members. Before joining ISKCON, Dhananjai was not a member of any religious group but was searching for a means of understanding the world and our role in it. He is active in spreading the teachings of Krishna through the activities of ISKCON and with other members of the group goes out into the city to perform **kirtan**, singing and chanting Krishna's name, and to talk to young people.

Dhananjai says: "My favourite story is the one about Krishna and the Sidhan **brahmin**. Although the *brahmin* and his wife are very poor, the *brahmin* is happy to continue to live as they do and accept their condition as part of the divine plan but his wife is very insistent that he should petition Lord Krishna for help. She points out to her husband that Krishna always responds and will not disappoint them if only her husband will ask. The *brahmin* decides that he will go to Krishna, not because he really wants anything but because it will give him a chance to meet his Lord. He gets a handful of cheap rice from a neighbour, as he has nothing of his own to take as a gift, and sets out on his journey.

The *brahmin* arrives at the opulent palace at Dwarka and Krishna rushes out to embrace him. Krishna treats the *brahmin* as an honoured guest and even performs **arti** much to the consternation of the other palace residents. The *brahmin* does not ask for anything but Krishna knows the purpose behind his journey and asks, "Have you brought something for me?" The *brahmin* is ashamed of the handful of poor rice he has brought and says he has nothing, but Krishna grabs it and eats it. He tells the *brahmin* that he will get more wealth than the god Indra in this life and the next.

Worshipping at a shrine of Krishna and Radha.

After one day the *brahmin* returns, completely satisfied by having simply seen Krishna, but he cannot find his village. Where the village was is now a great city and his wife is now as rich as the goddess **Lakshmi**. The *brahmin* realises that this is Krishna's work and vows that all his new prosperity will be used in the service of the Lord.

I like this story because it shows the characteristics of a true devotee in its teaching that we should use worldly things in the service of God. I don't think it is a myth. The stories of Krishna's power are amazing and instructive; they are true stories. Many are found in the *Bhagavata Purana*. If you give something, however small, it is returned a hundred times over by the Lord Krishna. In our society, devotion to God is seen as being a servant and therefore inferior. But being a devotee does not mean that you are exploited; even some Hindus do not find the idea of following Krishna in this way

A small shrine to the woman saint, Meera (15th century), who, according to tradition, merged with an image of Krishna.

attractive any more. The life of our founder shows that removing luxury can be a good thing because it makes you more dependent on Krishna and so more able to benefit from his generosity. Unfortunately, materialistic people are more likely to become atheists when things are taken away from them.

Krishna is the supreme Lord; all the *avataras* or descents of God are actually expansions of Krishna which means "to attract", so he is acting out what is possible for us so that we will be drawn to him. Young people can learn from Krishna that God is attractive and enjoyable, not stern, remote and boring. He is not interested in calling us to account for our good and bad deeds; to think like this is to bring God down to our own level. No matter what people do, Krishna cares for and loves them. He is a guide and support who offers us an alternative reality".

Krishan Kant Attri

> Krishan Kant Attri is the *pandit* (priest) based at the *mandir* in Newcastle upon Tyne. He was born in Bihar State in India and received a traditional education as a *sisya* (pupil) of an important guru. With his wife and young family he works to serve the local Hindu community and visitors who travel to the *mandir* from all over the region. Krishan Kant is active in spreading understanding about the Hindu tradition to young people, Hindus and non-Hindus, and frequently welcomes parties of school children into the *mandir*. The *mandir*, as is often the case in England, is not dedicated to any one form of God and houses images of Shiva, Rama, and the goddess **Durga**, as well as Krishna.

Krishan Kant says: "It is difficult to pick out any one story of Krishna and say, "This is my favourite". In a way the whole character of Krishna is itself the story. Krishna's character is very striking and dramatic, it makes a powerful impact on us, and whilst the stories show that he is fully human in his moods and emotions, he is at the same time God. It is by studying his character that we can come to know him and know God. This is why there are so many stories of Krishna, stories beginning with his childhood and leading right up to his teaching to Arjuna in the *Bhagavad Gita* - it is so that people are able to choose a particular story according to their age, personality or level of understanding. Each story of Krishna has something important to teach us.

Krishna depicted as the essence of all deity.

Krishna is the latest *avatara* and he came to bring the teaching of the *Gita* so that we can understand the nature of righteousness and make decisions about how to act in the world. Rama, the previous *avatara*, sets an example of how we should behave, what we should do, which we can copy; but Krishna's character cannot be copied. We must listen to what he says, his teachings, and then we will grow in understanding. So, we may not be able to follow Krishna by emulating his character, doing what he did, but we can follow his teaching, especially the message of the *Gita*.

The *Gita* is accessible to everyone, whether they are Hindus or non-Hindus, and regardless of their status or degree of education. The story of Arjuna's dilemma and the advice of his charioteer, Krishna, has something to teach us all. Krishna's explanations in the *Gita* of *karma*, how to improve this world, and the nature of salvation, can be interpreted at different levels so that everyone may benefit. Krishna unites everyone by showing that distinctions are not relevant to the development of an everyday understanding of what we should do and how we should be in the world. At the same time, everything is there within the *Gita*, so that it can be revisited as understanding grows and new insights are gained.

Another important lesson we can learn from Krishna is not to be too narrowly focused and sectarian in our views and opinions. Distinctions between followers of Vishnu and followers of Shiva may express a preference but are not significant: the stripping away of distinctions in the pursuit of that which is ultimately significant is the deepest teaching of the *Gita*. Popular stories illustrate this same point.

One of the stories of Krishna's birth describes how Shiva travelled to visit the baby and pay his respects. Another story tells of a devotee of Krishna who loses some money in a muddy pool and calls upon Lord Shiva to help him find it. Shiva asks why a devotee of Krishna should be asking him for help. The man replies that Lord Krishna is too finely dressed to get muddy in a pool but Shiva in his ascetic's rags and ashes would not mind!"

A composite image of Vishnu and Shiva.

Conclusion

We have started this book by looking into what some devotees of Krishna think and feel about him. Though there are differences in their views, there are also many things in common. They all find him immensely attractive and accessible for a variety of reasons, they all believe that he gives us a defining insight into God, they all derive practical lessons from their devotion to him and wish to make him better known to their families, friends and wider communities, and they all look specially towards one or both of the following source-texts for their knowledge of Krishna and of our relationship to him and to each other: the *Bhagavad Gita* and the *Bhagavata Purana*. This chapter provides a good basis for our continuing inquiry into the meaning of Krishna and his stories in what follows.

Questions to ask yourself:

1) Which story or stories of Krishna do you like the best, and why? Is it important that these stories should be believed to have actually happened? Explain your answer.

2) What do his followers see as distinctive of Krishna?

3) From the accounts of Krishna's devotees in this chapter, what do you think are Krishna's most attractive qualities? Give reasons for your answer.

Chapter 2
Sources for the Stories of Krishna

The *Bhagavata Purana:* Playful Devotion

The *Bhagavata Purana* is a long and famous text, produced in its present form probably in south India in about 9th century C.E. Among other things, it tells the story of Krishna's life through a series of incidents which demonstrate his playfulness and power. At first, he seems an ordinary child or youth who plays tricks on his friends and family; yet, as we have seen from the last chapter, each incident carries a deeper meaning and often ends with a super-human act of salvation. You will recall from the statements of Krishna's followers that the *Bhagavata Purana* is one of the most important sources of information about Krishna for them.

Stories of the infant Krishna stealing butter from his neighbours in the village or as a youth playing in the forest as he herds the cows show an engaging and very human

Main shrines at the Radhakrishna temple, Withington, Manchester.

character. Whilst such stories draw us close to Krishna, we are reminded of his power when, for example, his foster mother Yashoda looks into the child's mouth to check if he has been eating clay and sees the whole universe including herself contained therein!

Krishna's father and mother were Vasudeva and Devaki, the latter a relative of Kamsa, the tyrant king of the Yadavas, but stories of his birth explain that in fact God Vishnu descended as the eighth child of the couple to become Krishna in order to overcome tyranny. Kamsa hears of a prophecy that he will die at the hands of a child of Vasudeva. So Krishna is taken from his real parents and along with his elder brother Baladeva (also called Balarama) is brought up as the child of a cowherd, Nanda, and his wife, Yashoda, in the nearby forest of Gokula (and later in Vrndavan). Kamsa orders the destruction of all male infants but Krishna escapes.

Nanda and Yashoda bring up Krishna and his brother as their own children and he grows up to become a cowherd. The accounts of Krishna's adventures with the milkmaids (*gopis*) develop the theme of his playfulness and charm whilst also modelling the ideal relationship between the devotee and God. Many stories are told about the courtship of the *gopis* by Krishna, describing how he teases them, leading them to forget everything in the games and dances in the forest. The *Bhagavata Purana* shows how this love is transformed into pure devotion (**bhakti**). Stories in later books like the poem *Gitagovinda*, written in the 12th century, focus on the relationship between Krishna and one of the *gopis* called **Radha** to show how we should be devoted to God.

Eventually, the tyrant king Kamsa discovers where Krishna is and hatches a plot to lure him to his capital, Mathura, so that he can kill him. Kamsa's messenger falls victim to Krishna's charm and tells him about the plot but Krishna still agrees to make the journey to Mathura. The stories relate many exploits of Krishna leading up to the killing of Kamsa and the reunion with his true parents. Krishna now takes his proper place as a Yadava prince with a palace at Dwarka and a wife, Rukmini. In the course of time he has many adventures and acquires other wives according to the custom of a princely ruler of the Yadava clan.

Krishna rules the kingdom well until he is invited by the gods Shiva and **Brahma** to give up his earthly life and return to them. He dies when a hunter, mistaking his foot for part of a deer, shoots him. The hunter is armed with an arrow tipped with iron from a

The attraction of Krishna's divine melody

club made by priests to punish the Yadavas for a prank played on them by some disrespectful youths. Soon after Krishna's death, the kingdom of Dwarka is destroyed in a flood.

Krishna is generally regarded as an *avatara* of the supreme being, Vishnu. *Avatara* means "crossing over", and it is believed that Vishnu has taken a number of different forms, including that of the Buddha, in order to bring order to the world and set right conditions for people to perform their duty. Many followers of Krishna believe him to be the supreme being himself, **Bhagavan**. We can also find evidence to support the existence of a historical Krishna, sometimes called Vasudeva Krishna, the leader of a northern Indian clan.

True Devotion or *Bhakti*

Bhakti is practised through worship, the giving of offerings and the performance of one's *dharma*, and ideally it is the sincerity of these activities that is important not the status of the worshipper or the size of the offering. Privilege arising from caste is not generally maintained in the *bhakti* tradition. Worship in the *Bhagavata Purana* is not directly based on traditional Vedic ceremonies. More emphasis is put on group activities such as singing, dancing and the recitation of stories.

The *Bhagavata Purana* says that "Vishnu is pleased when all the distressed, the blind, and the pitiable have eaten" (8.16.56). Sometimes the emphasis on poverty and humility is so strong that there is a suggestion that only the poor can ever be true devotees but this is not the central teaching of the *Bhagavata Purana*. *Dharma* is still linked to caste but a distinction is made between the social position and the qualities of the person; to be worthy of respect, a *brahmin* must embody the appropriate qualities. Nineteenth-century Hindu reformers, including Vivekananda, took up this idea in their re-interpretation of the caste system.

The *Bhagavad Gita*: Arjuna's Dilemma and our Dilemmas

Arjuna's Dilemma

The *Bhagavad Gita* is a small but very important part of the famous epic, the *Mahabharata*, and is thought to have been composed about the beginning of the

Devotees at a shrine of Krishna.

Common Era, give or take a century or two. It opens with two mighty armies drawn up for battle on the field of Kurukshetra in north India. On one side are ranked the Kauravas, the hundred sons of the king, Dhritarasthra, led by the eldest brother Duryodhana, and their cohorts, and on the other side stand the Pandavas, the five sons of Pandu, led by their eldest brother Yudhisthira. Dhritarasthra and Pandu are brothers, so the battle is a civil war.

The younger brother of Yudhisthira is Arjuna, and the first chapter of the *Gita* describes how he waits in his chariot in the ranks of the Pandavas for the battle to commence. Arjuna is a hero and a great archer, but he is troubled by the thought of fighting his friends and relatives. When the signal to advance is given, Arjuna orders Krishna, his charioteer, to stop his chariot in front of the opposing armies, and as he surveys the enemy lines he falls into despair:

"There Arjuna saw, standing their ground, fathers, grandfathers, teachers, maternal uncles, brothers, sons, grandsons, friends..." He speaks these words to Krishna: "When I see these my own people eager to fight, on the brink, my limbs grow heavy, and my mouth is parched, my body trembles and my hair bristles....I can no longer stand - my mind is reeling. Nothing good can come from slaughtering one's own family in battle". (Johnson, 2.26-31)

This then is the crux of Arjuna's dilemma: as a **kshatriya** or member of the ruling warrior class, it is his duty to fight but he cannot kill his relatives and friends.

Yudhisthira, the leader of the Pandavas, was tricked out of his inheritance by the Kauravas in a game of dice. Under the terms agreed with Duryodhana, he was to regain his kingdom after serving thirteen years in exile with his brothers and their wife. However, when the Pandavas returned from exile to reclaim the kingdom, Duryodhana refused to honour the agreement and Yudhisthira, reluctantly, declared war.

Arjuna is caught between conflicting codes of values: his duty as a *kshatriya*, and a Pandava, is to fight, but killing one's kin and waging a civil war and damaging the social order in the kingdom is also wrong. Also, Arjuna doubts whether material gain, even the winning of a kingdom, can justify slaughter.

Fulfilling one's duty (*dharma*) is not simply a matter of maintaining the social order. There is a link with the cosmic order and this is explored through Arjuna's charioteer. Krishna in the *Mahabharata* is portrayed as both a friendly neighbour of the Pandavas and (in the *Gita*) as an *avatara*, the manifestation of the supreme Lord. Yudhisthira sends Krishna as an envoy to the Kauravas but his attempts to reconcile the two sides fail. Krishna then offers the combatants a choice between having his army or himself on their side in the battle. Duryodhana chooses the army and Arjuna chooses Krishna to act as his charioteer. Essentially, this choice is between the ways of humans or the ways of God, and in the *Gita* Krishna advises Arjuna as he struggles to understand his *dharma* and resolve his dilemma.

Today the *Gita* is available in numerous translations, many commentators have interpreted its teachings and the events on the battlefield at Kurukshetra are portrayed in film, video and picture-books. Jean-Claude Carriere, the screenwriter for Peter Brook's film version of the epic, interprets the story as the Great History of Mankind, and

Scenes from the life of Krishna.

refers to a popular Indian saying to the effect that:

> "What is worth finding anywhere else can be found in the *Mahabharata*. But what is not found in the *Mahabharata* is not worth finding anywhere else".

The Teachings of the *Gita*

The story of the *Gita* is woven around Krishna's attempts to persuade Arjuna that he must take up his bow and fight the Kauravas. In the first chapter we saw how important the teachings of the *Gita* are to many of Krishna's followers. In the *Gita* Arjuna's doubts and fears, which reflect our own problems as we journey through life, are explored and each chapter takes a particular focus. The *Gita* is practical in its attitude to the search for truth; understanding is sought not for its own sake but because it will lead to salvation. The teachings of the *Gita* aim to resolve the apparent tension between *dharma* and *moksha* (duty and salvation), and demonstrate the saving grace of devotion to God. Through his conversation with Krishna, Arjuna comes to a better understanding of the self and the nature of action. In Chapter 11, Arjuna has a vision of Krishna in his true form as the supreme Lord and, although he is terrified, he sees the power and grace of God.

> The Lord said:
> "I am time run on, destroyer of the universe, risen here to annihilate worlds. Regardless of you, all these warriors, stationed in opposing ranks, shall cease to exist......They have already been hewn down by me: Arjuna, simply be the instrument" (11.32-33)

> Krishna continues by reassuring Arjuna:
> "This form of mine, which you have seen, is very hard to see. Even the gods crave incessantly for a glimpse of this form. Neither through the Vedas, nor through asceticism, neither by alms-giving, nor by sacrifice is it possible to see me in the way you have seen me. But by exclusive devotion, Arjuna, I can be known and seen thus, as I really am, and entered into......He who acts for me, who makes me the highest goal, who is devoted to me, who has abandoned attachment, who is without hatred for any being, comes to me....." (11.52-55).

Symbols of the presence of the guru.

Arjuna's situation is a genuine dilemma because he is free to choose between two courses of action: to fight or not to fight. At the end of his dialogue with Krishna, Arjuna is still free to choose but he has a better understanding of the nature of that choice. Arjuna realises that he is caught up in a chain of events. The solution is not to avoid performing his duty but by exercising self-discipline to develop the right intentions.

Krishna in the *Gita* teaches a *practical* morality that equips the man of action, Arjuna, to fulfill his proper role in society. This idea was repeated on several occasions in the statements made in the first chapter of the book. Ego is an irrelevance and everything that is good is achieved through self-less action (**nishkama karma**) and devotion to Krishna. The lessons are learned through a poem - the *Gita* - that draws as much upon our emotions and imagination as it does upon reason, and this too is part of the lesson Krishna is teaching.

Our Dilemmas

The popularity of the *Gita* lies in its relevance to the problems we all encounter in our daily lives. Any thoughtful person poses the questions that Arjuna asks in the *Gita* - although most of us are fortunate enough not to have to do so from the front line of a civil war!

We cannot know what the actual consequences of even our best intentions may be. The price of our freedom as individuals is that we face choices that we are unable to resolve from our limited perspectives. The values we hold and our ambitions frequently come into conflict and most decisions are not choices between right and wrong, which would be relatively straightforward.

Sections of the *Gita* seem to suggest that we are not free. So Krishna says at one point: "Arjuna, in the centre of the heart of all beings their lord stands still, mechanically revolving all creatures through his magical power" (18.61).

A stall selling devotional pictures of Krishna.

In one sense this is true: we have little influence over the laws of material nature. But Arjuna learns that whilst what he has always considered to be his self, his personality and everyday experience cannot be free from the laws of causation and social ties, his realised self is beyond ego and attachment and so is completely free.

Real ethics begin when values clash. In contemporary, modern societies exploring the ultimate source of the values we hold is difficult when there is no agreed set of beliefs and ethical dilemmas are hard to resolve. Krishna in the *Gita* leads us to the point at which human understanding is exhausted and then he invites us to devote ourselves to God. For many people, it is the description of the link between intention and action in the *Gita* which is most helpful in their struggle to overcome their selfishness and make sense of the world.

The Paradox of Krishna

Stories of Krishna are told during the festival of Holi: a time of wild celebration and near anarchy when social conventions are turned upside down. Holi is a time of reckoning for the mighty when, as part of the festivities, the community's elder statesmen find themselves being covered in mud or coloured powders by people who would normally show them every respect. Women who would not usually challenge the authority of their husbands or fathers may take to the streets with sticks and beat any men they meet mercilessly! Children feel free to play practical jokes on their parents and teachers with no fear of punishment. Guided by Krishna each person assumes the role of his or her opposite:

> "Each actor playfully takes the role of others in relation to his [or her] own usual self. Each may thereby learn to play his [or her] own routine roles afresh, surely with renewed understanding, possibly with greater grace, perhaps with a reciprocating love." (McKim Marriot, in Singer 1968:212)

During the rest of the year, devotees of Krishna often meet to participate in group worship which includes devotional singing (called *kirtan* or **bhajan**), where discriminations of caste and gender are supposed to be ignored. The normally very orthodox Smarta Brahmins in Madras participate fully in *bhajans* with low-caste devotees. In recent years there has been an increase in the participation of middle-class, Western-educated Hindus in this kind of devotion. It may be that in an increasingly materialistic modern society, *bhakti* offers a path to salvation which is more accessible even to those groups who in the past may have followed more philosophical systems such as **Advaita** Vedanta.

Krishna plays with opposites; he is the practical joker but also the upholder of *dharma* who helps his followers to fulfill their duty. He is human and yet he is the supreme Lord. At the same time, Krishna reconciles all opposites by showing that the distinctions on which they are based are mere surface impressions and have no ultimate reality. Krishna is the essence (*vibhuti*) of everything, the gambling of rogues as well as the wisdom of the sages, as he tells Arjuna in chapter 10 of the *Gita*.

The playful approach to duty and compassionate love demonstrated by Krishna in the *Bhagavata Purana* is a message which has as much relevance today as it did when it was first composed. *The Krishna of Vrindaban is the antidote to pomposity, self-righteousness and a religious spirit that takes itself too seriously.* Krishna reminds us of our responsibilities and expects people to contribute to a well-ordered society by putting others before themselves. He also reminds us that God's creation is ours to enjoy responsibly, and that being religious should also be fun!

Chapter 3
Questions for Today

1. What is our dharma?

The importance of *dharma* or right conduct is emphasised in all the stories of Krishna. No one can evade their *dharma*, as Arjuna found on the battlefield of Kurukshetra, and it is by the proper performance of our *dharma* that we will become better people. We need to understand our duties and responsibilities so that we can make a full contribution to society whilst not becoming bound by our egos and preoccupied with material concerns. Krishna's teachings will help us reach this better understanding of our *dharma*. On one level this all appears relatively straightforward, even more so when we remember that we can surrender ourselves to God in total devotion and so be helped directly. But problems naturally arise when we question the existing social order.

In traditional societies, roles and responsibilities changed slowly, if at all, and social positions were fixed. Whilst Krishna overturns conventions from time to time, he does so within the overarching framework of *dharma*. The anarchy of the festival of Holi lasts only a few days before everything returns to normal and once again the maintenance of social order is placed above individualistic self-expression. Modern society is characterised by rapid change and the re-definition of social roles and responsibilities.

The challenge today is to continue to have a respect for the performance of duty whilst looking for a way of reinterpreting dharma in the light of changing circumstances.

Do the stories of Krishna teach us to change our minds or to change the world - or is this a question based on the false distinctions he warned about?

2. How free are we?

The stories of Krishna encourage devoted service and this can seem to be at odds with contemporary values which promote individualism. The tension between free expression and social conformity is explored through the paradox of Krishna. The essential teaching of Krishna is that as personalities with bodies and egos our freedom is limited by the constraints of material nature and the law of **karma**. True freedom lies

The intimacy of Radha and Krishna.

in understanding our real selves which are not reducible to the material world and its forces, and so need not be overwhelmed by the laws of cause and effect.

The stories sometimes appear to show that our actions are pre-determined and we can in fact do little to alter a course of events. Arjuna is told that whether he chooses to fight or not, the people in the battle will be killed; indeed, they have already been killed by Krishna as supreme Lord! What does this mean, and how do we avoid adopting a passive and fatalistic attitude to life?

Would we be justified in saying that it doesn't matter what we do because it has all been decided beforehand? The answer to this question has to be that taking such a negative attitude is wrong, as we are expected to continue to act purposefully and fulfill our *dharma*. Nevertheless, it does seem to inhibit spontaneous and creative action beyond our prescribed *dharma*. But we may still ask: is this necessarily the case?

Critics of Hinduism have focused on this issue in their analysis of the part played by religion in preventing material development and social progress in India. The criticisms have, in the main, been unjust and selective in their interpretation of tradition. It is easy to misrepresent Krishna's teaching and destroy the spirit of what is being said. The stories do encourage action, and their playfulness or spirit of *lila* is a teaching about true *spontaneity*, and the *transience* or *contingency* of worldly things. Thus there is also a realism about the limits of human action.

"How free am I?" is a question we all must address, and the stories of Krishna show one way of thinking about it whilst leaving us free to reach our own conclusions.

Do we need to "kill" our gurus?

If we take things only at face value, then the *gopis* were unfaithful to their husbands in their pursuit of Krishna, and Arjuna will be responsible for the deaths of the teachers he respects if he fights the battle. Central to the paradox of Krishna is the idea that devotion to God requires the overturning of social conventions, and yet the purpose of *avataras* is generally the restoration of *dharma*.

Krishna's stories encourage us to examine conventions critically and take more

Chaitanya (15th-16th Century), regarded by some as the embodiment of Radha and Krishna, heals someone suffering from leprosy.

responsibility by making choices. *Tradition and dharma are not necessarily the same thing and it is not enough always simply to do whatever everyone else does or has done in the past.*

Krishna advocates devotion (*bhakti*) as a means of overcoming our selfish egoism and so being able to follow a path of action which will be pure and appropriate. "Killing our gurus", the striking phrase used by Dr Anand in chapter 1, may mean being prepared to abandon cherished views or opinions. Alternatively, we may need to "kill our gurus" in the sense of being prepared to take responsibility for any decision we make, and not blame someone else, even though they may have authority over us, for what has happened.

Chapter 4
Further information

In this chapter we shall consider further information about sources for our knowledge and understanding of Krishna. This will help us to go deeper into the tradition and to catch something of the great richness and complexity of the history and transmission of awareness of Krishna.

The earliest certain reference to the Krishna we have been speaking about is in a scripture called the *Chandogya Upanishad*, which can be dated to about 7th century B.C.E. According to the theological schools called the Vedanta, the most authoritative *Upanishads* (whose dates range from about the eighth century B.C.E. to about the second century C.E.) express deep spiritual experiences of the nature of reality and the means of acquiring the knowledge that will make us free from the ties of the material world. For these schools and for many other Hindus, the *Upanishads* are called *vedanta* because they are seen as the "end of the *Vedas*" (which is what *vedanta* means) in so far as they offer a conclusive statement on previous teaching.

The *Mahabharata*, (about 400 B.C.E. - about 400 C.E.), which we have mentioned before, is the next source of information about Krishna. It is within the *Mahabharata* that we find the *Bhagavad Gita*, which contains the famous teachings of Krishna as supreme Lord to his warrior-friend, Arjuna. As a sort of very long Appendix to the *Mahabharata*, is a text called the *Harivamsa* (datable to about 3rd-4th century C.E.) which relates important stories about the young Krishna. "Hari" is a popular title for Krishna.

The *Vishnu Purana* (about 4th-5th century C.E. in its present form), a large text containing a great deal of different kinds of information, is our next source. The *Puranas* are a group of Sanskrit texts which contain well-known narratives among much other material. The *Bhagavata Purana* (about 9th century C.E.) is the next major source of information about Krishna. It is given special reverence by a number of important Hindu groups, including the Hare Krishnas. Finally, poems composed by devotees of Krishna elaborate on themes drawn from the various sources mentioned above. The Sanskrit poem, *Gitagovinda*, written by Jayadeva in 12th century, is very well-known

Radha in search of Krishna.

and has been very influential in shaping a form of Krishna-devotion in which Krishna's partner Radha plays a central part, *but there are many other poems* composed in various regional languages that are part of the treasure-store of ongoing devotion to Krishna.

The *Bhagavad Gita*

The oldest surviving *commentary* on the *Gita* is that of the great theologian Shankara, composed probably in the 9th century C.E. The Gita has since become an extremely popular religious text with numerous commentaries, interpretations and latter-day translations. The *Gita* has attracted the attention of Hindu reformers in this and the last century because it was seen to offer a model of the perfect man of action, called the **karma-yogi**, which could withstand the criticisms of western, Christian missionaries, and social reformers.

An important interpreter of Krishna in 19th century was the Bengali, Bankim Chandra Chatterjee (1838-1894), who was influenced by the Positivist thought of the French philosopher, Auguste Comte. The Positivists thought that religious belief and practice were important because they encouraged societies to work together for a common aim and furthered human development by providing good role models. Bankim's interpretation of Hinduism has been described as a Positivist reform. In his book, the *Essentials of Dharma*, Bankim describes religion as a system designed to promote full human development, that is, culture. However, he says that Hinduism is superior to Comte's so-called Religion of Humanity in achieving this aim because God, in the form of Krishna, is a better role-model than any purely human hero. Bankim was not comfortable with the sentimental and mythological view of Krishna he said existed in the *Puranas*. If Krishna was to symbolise the perfect man, he said, everything he did must be humanly possible. Some critics of Bankim have argued that though he rejects Comte's Religion of Humanity as a poor substitute for the worship of God, his representation of Krishna results in God becoming more human than divine (see Forbes 1975:135).

Another very influential interpreter of Krishna was Swami Vivekananda (1863-1902). Vivekananda's interest in Krishna did not develop until comparatively late in his life, but he promoted the *Gita* from the very beginning of his writings. He mentioned the *Gita* as the proclaimer of universal religion at the Parliament of Religions held in Chicago in 1893, which took the westernised religious world by storm. Even before his departure for the West, he encouraged daily reading of the text.

For Vivekananda, the *Gita* is important as a source of teachings, among other things, on Karma Yoga, that is, the path of selfless disciplined action. We saw in chapter 1 how the *Gita* is seen as providing this ideal for modern living. From Vivekananda's comments on the *Gita*, it is plain that he admires most of all its robust outlook and call to action. Even so, Vivekananda recommends the building up of a little muscle before approaching the *Gita*, and in one of his more well-known declarations he proclaims: "First of all, our young men must be strong. Religion will come afterwards.....You will understand the *Gita* better with your biceps, your muscles, a little stronger" (*Collected Works*, II:242).

The *Gita*, according to Vivekananda, is part of the continual struggle in India between the *kshatriyas* and the *brahmins*, that is, the ruling and the priestly classes respectively. Yet he believed that the teachings of the *Gita* can be followed by everyone. Like Bankim he was less comfortable with the Krishna of the Puranic tradition, questioning the historical validity of some of the stories. He suggested that they might have little value in modern India. He was writing at the time of the developing nationalist movement in India against British colonial rule, when a number of the nationalists thought that role-models in the form of stern warriors or teachers would be especially useful. Yet there were other views of Krishna both as a role-model and an object of devotion; thus Vivekananda's opposition to the portrayal of Krishna as a boy and a young man marks him out from contemporaries such as Keshab Chandra Sen (1838-1884) who thought that the *bhakti* tradition was very relevant to the modern world. We have seen that both emphases come through in the statements made in chapter 1.

Western scholars were very interested in the *Gita*; it was one of the first Sanskrit religious texts to be introduced into Europe and was translated into English by Charles Wilkins in 1785. The poet Edwin Arnold published a very popular version, called *The Song Celestial*, which was distributed widely by the Theosophical Society. Some Western commentators were struck by the apparent similarities between the teacher Krishna and Christ as saviour-figures and embodiments of God. The *Gita* was often described as the "Bible" or "Gospel" of Hinduism by both Western and Hindu writers.

M. K. Gandhi, called the "Mahatma" or "great-souled one", the great Indian reformer and political leader of the twentieth century, found the *Gita* to be a source of inspiration for his own work, and he confessed that he first read it in English whilst training to be a lawyer in London. The fact that a text centred on a battlefield influenced Gandhi who is most famous for his teachings on non-violence shows the scope of interpretation made possible in the *Gita*.

Can you find ways of understanding how this can be so?

The *Bhagavata Purana*

"Purana" literally means "something old or ancient", and the word distinguishes these compositions from another category known as *itihasa* or "happenings". The *Mahabharata*, for instance, is classed as *itihasa*. But the distinction is not very clear, and the *Puranas* form an encyclopaedic blend of ancient and medieval Hinduism including religious, philosophical, theological, social and political thought. The *Bhagavata Purana* is a fairly late example of the Puranic tradition and is considered to be one of the finest. This *Purana*, especially its most famous section, Book 10, which deals with Krishna's youthful exploits, has been described as the most enchanting poem ever written:

> "In his [the poet's] pages the world appears as a magic land where every object, if only it is rightly seen, is a key to truth and to eternity" (Singer, 1968:vii)

We have seen that it is a Sanskrit text datable to about the ninth century C.E. in its present form, originating probably in the Tamil country in south India. It contains different kinds of material blended to proclaim the divine supremacy of Krishna. Its popularity caused it to spread across India, and by 1895 there were 136 listed commentaries. The oldest known commentary is that of Sridhara Swami who was a follower of the Advaita Vedanta tradition. One of the more recent is that of Swami Prabhupada, the founder of the International Society for Krishna Consciousness (ISKCON), a devotional form of Hinduism. Like the *Gita*, one of the characteristics of the *Bhagavata Purana* has been its ability to accommodate a wide scope of interpretation.

The story of how the *Bhagavata* first came to the West is an interesting one. It

Chaitanya as the embodiment of Radha and Krishna

begins with a south Indian interpreter in the mid-eighteenth century who translated a Tamil summary of the original Sanskrit text into French for some gentlemen in Pondicherry (the former French territory on the east coast of southern India). Back in France it came to the attention of the man of letters, Voltaire, who was interested in its ideas, and it was eventually published anonymously in Paris in 1788. The meaning of the text had suffered in the transmission, and in 1840 the scholar Eugene Burnouf published a more accurate French translation closely followed by H H Wilson's English version (see Singer, 1968:viii).

In the sixteenth century a very influential devotee of Krishna was the mystic Chaitanya. **Chaitanya** developed a special consciousness of Krishna which included his gopi-partner, Radha, as his female divine counterpart. Chaitanya was deeply influenced by the *Bhagavata Purana*, and many of his followers, who include the Gaudiya **Vaishnavas**, believe that he was an embodiment of Radha and Krishna himself. In the West, Gaudiyas include the Hare Krishnas, who practise a form of devotion to Krishna and Radha which includes vegetarianism, an appreciation of the beauties of nature, and ecstatic singing and dancing.

In the nineteenth century, both the *Bhagavad Gita* and the *Bhagavata Purana* played an important part, each in its own way, in developing a new sense of devotion to Krishna and in renewing interest among Indian nationalists in *bhakti* as a means of gaining self-belief and regenerating India. This is sometimes called the Neo-Krishna movement, and gave rise to a trend among Indians to proclaim the glories of Krishna anew not only in their own land but also with considerable success abroad. As we have seen, e.g. by reference to contemporary devotional groups, this trend continues to the present day.

A Note for Teachers

The title of the book *Stories of Krishna* highlights the need to explore diversity when approaching this key figure in the Hindu tradition whilst at the same time considering the unifying themes and concepts. The book is best used with pupils who already have some knowledge and understanding of aspects of Krishna which can provide a foundation from which to enjoy the different perspectives offered in the interviews. Possible course units: the use of story to convey values; the creative tension that often exists between sets of values and how these might be resolved; how different members of a faith approach core stories and make them meaningful in their own lives. A key point to draw out would be the need to engage with stories and ask the questions what does this mean to the person being interviewed and what does this mean to me? Working with the book in this way would encompass learning about Krishna in the Hindu tradition and learning from the stories: two key aspects of many programmes of study in RE.

Suggestions for use:

1) Groups of pupils could be allocated different interviews to read and discuss. They could then prepare a short presentation of the key ideas expressed by the person in the interview. In a plenary session points of similarity could be identified.

2) The teacher (or a pupil) could take the 'hot seat' and answer questions from the point of view of one of the people interviewed.

3) Follow-up questions arising from discussions of the themes identified in the book could be explored with a visitor to the class or, where this is not practical, by letter or e-mail.

4) The key questions identified in the book would lend themselves to further research both within the wider Hindu tradition (the section on further information could be used as a starting point) but also as experimental questions to be explored from different religious and secular perspectives.

5) Pupils could carry out their own interviews of children in their own class or a parallel class or group to retell their favourite story of Krishna and say what it means to them. Cross phase interviews with younger or older pupils could provide a wide range of views.

Glossary

Advaita   "non-duality", or school that teaches that change and difference are superficial and illusory and that the goal of life is to realise our ultimate oneness (or non-duality) with the pure and indivisible supreme Reality, called Brahman, existing below the surface of being.

arti: a ritual in which a flame is waved in a circular motion from left to right in front of someone to show them honour and respect.

avatar(a):   "embodied descent", usually of deity into human affairs.

B.C.E.:   Before the Common (or Christian) Era.

Bhagavan: "Adorable One", usually applied devotionally to God.

bhajan: devotional song to God.

bhakti: devotion, implying a desire to share the life of the loved one.

Brahma: name of God in his creative function (to be distinguished from Brahman, the name of God as the supreme Reality).

brahmin: anglicised form of the Sanskrit term *brahmana*, referring to the priestly order in society; the highest caste.

C.E.:   Common (or Christian) Era.

Chaitanya: 16th century saint of devotion to God, believed by some to be also a descent of God.

dharma: quality, attribute, proper order, right conduct, virtue, duty.

Durga: name of the Goddess as destroyer of evildoers.

Gita: (also Bhagavad Gita) sacred text (about beginning of the common era), and part of the *Mahabharata*, recounting a conversation between the supreme being, Krishna, and his friend and disciple, Arjuna, about righteous living (*dhartma*) and salvation.

gopis: cowherdess companions of the youthful Krishna.

jnana: knowledge (in religious contexts: spiritual, insightful, knowledge).

karman/karma: action, deed; "karma" is also the consequence of self-centred deeds that bear good or bad fruit, that is, pleasant or unpleasant experiences or situations, in some future state or life (see also **nishkama karma**).

karma-yogi: follower of a disciplined path of selfless action.

kirtan: devotional song praising God.

kshatriya: member of the warrior order or caste of society.

Lakshmi: The Goddess, in her form of bestowing wealth and prosperity.

lila: Gods so-called playfulness; in fact, the display of God's unconventionality; the divine spontaneity, showing that worldly rules are not ultimately important.

mandir: temple

moksha: liberation from **samsara**.

nishkama karma: selfless action; action that does not generate fresh karma.

prasad: an offering made in ritual worship to God which is then filled with God's blessing for sharing with others.

Purana:	ancient sacred writings containing stories about religious figures and events and a wide range of other data.
Radha:	Krishna's favourite **gopi**.
Ram(a):	an **avatar** of God **Vishnu**, husband of **Sita**, and king of Ayodhya.
Ravan(a):	ogre-king of the island, Lanka, and abductor of **Sita**.
samsara:	the round of rebirth.
Sanskrit:	the ancient language of Hindu scripture and learning.
Shiva:	one form of God; also, the preferred name of God for many Hindus (i.e. those who are Shaivites).
shruti:	another name for **Veda**.
Sita:	wife of **Ram(a)**; generally regarded as the model of a wife.
smriti:	authoritative texts which help us understand **dharma** and **shruti**.
Sudra:	member of the fourth or serving order or caste of society.
Upanishads:	sacred texts teaching about the existence and nature of the supreme being, and forming the end of the **Veda**.
Vaishnava:	follower of or having to do with **Vishnu**.
Veda:	ancient Hindu scriptures in Sanskrit.
Vishnu:	a form of God; also, for many Hindus the preferred name of God (i.e. for Vaishnavites).
yoga:	method of disciplining and uniting mind and body.

Select Sources of Information

Archer, W.G., 1957:   *The Loves of Krishna*,
Macmillan, New York.

Basham, A.L., 1967:   *The Wonder that was India*,
Sidgwick & Jackson, London.

Baumfield, V.M., 1991:   *Swami Vivekananda's Practical Vedanta*,
Unpublished PhD thesis,
University of Newcastle upon Tyne.

Bhaktivedanta, A.C., 1993:   *Krsna: The Supreme Personality of Godhead*,
(Swami Prabhupada)   The Bhaktivedanta Book Trust, Borehamwood, Herts.

Chatterjee, B.C., 1977:   *Dharmatattva (Essentials of Dharma)*,
(Translated by   Sribhumi Publishing Co., Calcutta.
Manomohan Ghosh)

Dimock, E.C.,   *In Praise of Krishna: Songs from the Bengali*,
& Levertov D., 1967 ed: Anchor Books, Doubleday & Co., New York.

Eck, Diana, 1996 ed.:   *Darsan: Seeing the Divine Image in India*,
(2nd revised ed.)   Columbia University Press, New York.

Edgerton, F., 1974:   *The Bhagavad Gita*,
Harvard University Press, Cambridge, Mass.

Farquhar, J.N., 1914:   *Modern Religious Movements in India*,
Oxford University Press.

Forbes, G.H., 1975:   *Positivism in Bengal*,
Minerva Associates, Calcutta.

Fuller, C.J., 1992: *The Camphor Flame: Popular Hinduism and Society in India*, Princeton University Press.

Jackson, R & Killingley, D, 1991: *Moral Issues in the Hindu Tradition*, Trentham Books, Stoke on Trent.

Johnson, W.J., 1994: *The Bhagavad Gita*, Oxford University Press.

Kinsley, D.R., 1979: *The Divine Player: A Study of Krsna Lila*, Motilal Banarsidass, Delhi.

Klostermaier, K., 1989: *A Survey of Hinduism*, State University of New York Press, Albany.

Knott, K, 1986: *My Sweet Lord*, Aquarian, Wellinborough.

Lipner, J, 1994:
(Paperback edition, 1998) *Hindus: Their Religious Beliefs and Practices*, Routledge, London.

O'Flaherty, W. D. (ed.), 1988: *Textual Sources for the Study of Hinduism*, Manchester University Press.

Parekh, B.M.C., 1969: *Shri Vallabhacharya: Life, Teachings and Movement*, Sri Bhagawata Dharma Mission, Rajkot, India.

Singer, M. (ed.), 1968: *Krishna: Myths, Rites and Attitudes*, University of Chicago Press edition.

Tagare, G.V., 1976: *The Bhagavata Purana*, Motilal Banarsidass, Delhi.

Zaehner, R.C., 1969: *The Bhagavad-Gita*, Oxford University Press.

Acknowledgements

The photographs on pp 13, 15 ,17, 19, 20, 28, 30, 34, 41, and 44 were taken by and /or reproduced by the kind permission of Dr. Jacqueline Suthren Hirst. Thanks to Dr. J. Lipner for the photographs on pp. 22, 27, 32, 39, and 43. The Lalit Kala Akademi, Rabindra Bhaban, New Delhi, is thanked for the reproductions on pp. 24, 25, 36, 37, 48, 49, 54 and 55. Every effort was made to obtain permission for these reproductions. We acknowledge with thanks permission from The Bhaktivedanta Book Trust International 1988 to reproduce the pictures on pp. 51 and 59. The publisher has sought to identify and contact the copyright holders of artistic work for permission. Any omissions will gladly be rectified in future reprints. The author would like to thank all those who helped in the making of this book, especially those who kindly agreed to be interviewed in Chapter 1. She would also like to thank the Hindu community in Newcastle for their support.

The dedication speaks for itself.